CHECKERBOARD HOW-TO LIBRARY

COOL CRAFTS

Cool Beaded Jewelry

Pam Scheunemann

ABDO
Publishing Company

visit us at
www.abdopub.com

Published by ABDO Publishing Company, 4940 Viking Drive, Edina, Minnesota 55435. Copyright ©
2005 by Abdo Consulting Group, Inc. International copyrights reserved in all countries. No part of this
book may be reproduced in any form without written permission from the publisher. Checkerboard Library
is a trademark and logo of ABDO Publishing Company.

Printed in the United States.

Design and Production: Mighty Media, Inc.
    Cover Photo: Anders Hanson
    Interior Photos: Anders Hanson
    Series Coordinator: Pam Scheunemann
    Editor: Pam Price
    Art Direction: Pam Scheunemann

Library of Congress Cataloging-in-Publication Data

Scheunemann, Pam, 1955-
    Cool beaded jewelry / Pam Scheunemann.
      p. cm. -- (Cool crafts)
    Includes index.
    ISBN 1-59197-739-8
    1. Beadwork--Juvenile literature. 2. Jewelry making--Juvenile literature. I. Title. II.
Series.

TT860.S34 2004
745.594'2--dc22
                                                                                    2004046292

Special thanks to Kari Erickson for supplying many of the beads shown.

⚠ For Your Safety
Some of the tools shown in this book should be used only when an adult is present.

Contents

Introduction 4

The History of Beads 5

Types of Beads 6

Basic Bead Shapes 10

Bead Sizes 11

Findings 12

Tools & Supplies 14

Designing with Beads 16

Memory Wire Bracelet 18

Necklace on a Cord 20

Beaded Necklace 22

Beaded Bracelet 24

Daisy Chain Necklace 26

Beaded Ring 28

Stretchy Bracelet 30

Glossary 31

Index 32

Boldfaced words throughout the text are defined in the glossary.

Introduction

There are a million kinds of beads and just as many ways to use them. The art of beading has recently gained popularity. There are bead shops, classes, magazines, books, and Web sites springing up all over the place. People of all ages are enjoying beads and beading.

This book will give you an overview of beading. It will show types of beads available. Simple tools used in making jewelry will be discussed. Some easy projects will provide a basis for you to create bead projects of your own. Hopefully, they will inspire you to explore the many uses of beads. They're not just for jewelry! Beads are used in many art forms. Examples are bead weaving, bead crochet, beaded wire crafts, and bead embroidery.

With the variety of beads available, you can really personalize your beadwork. You pick the colors, the shapes, the textures, and the style. It's all about what you like! Make some one-of-a-kind jewelry for yourself or make some for gifts.

The History of Beads

No matter what your age, beads have been around longer than you have. Archeologists have found beads approximately 40,000 years old! People all around the world have used beads for many purposes. Some uses are spiritual. Beads have also been used as money, as symbols of wealth, and for personal adornment.

People of early civilizations made beads from locally available materials. These materials included bone, wood, seeds, stones, and shells. Different beads were created in different parts of the world. As people began to travel to other areas, the materials and techniques for bead making traveled with them. Beads became a valuable trade item.

The glass bead plays an important role in the history of beads. People around the world have used glass seed beads for centuries. Explorers and traders introduced these colorful beads to many cultures. They were then adapted into the traditional dress and customs of these cultures.

Glass bead making has been a highly valued skill since its invention. Bead-making methods that were developed by Europeans are still in use today. Many of these techniques are secret and not to be disclosed by workers. Eventually, mass production made glass beads available to everyone.

People have been fascinated by beads ever since humans first put a shell or a bone on a string. The art of making and using beads remains popular throughout the world. Beads have brought the world closer together in ancient times and in the present.

Types of Beads

Almost every kind of material has been used for making beads. The beads shown here are only a small sampling of what is available. The important thing is to select beads that are appropriate for your specific project. Beyond that, the choice is limited only by your imagination!

Glass Beads

There are an endless variety of glass beads available. You can find almost any color, size, or shape you need.

People have been working with glass for the past 9,000 years. Many bead-making techniques have been established.

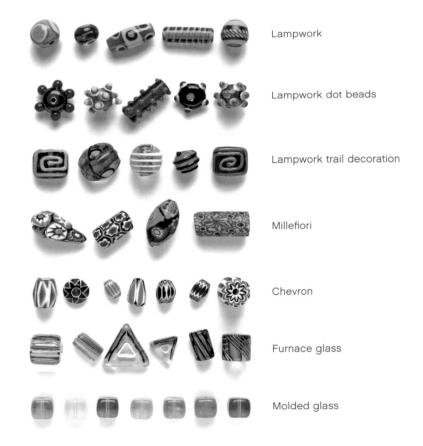

Lampwork

Lampwork dot beads

Lampwork trail decoration

Millefiori

Chevron

Furnace glass

Molded glass

Rocailles

Rocailles are tiny glass beads also known as seed beads. *Rocaille* is French for "little stone." They are used for jewelry making, embroidery, and embellishment on a variety of articles. They are made by slicing a long tube of glass into tiny beads. Rocailles come in many colors and finishes.

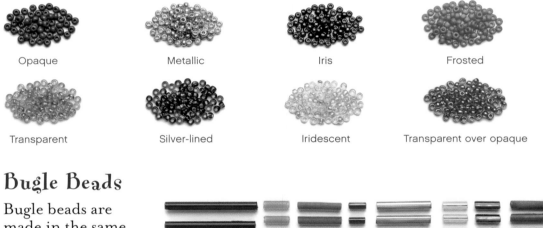

Opaque	Metallic	Iris	Frosted

Transparent	Silver-lined	Iridescent	Transparent over opaque

Bugle Beads

Bugle beads are made in the same way as rocailles. They are just sliced into longer pieces.

Swarovski Glass

In 1895, Daniel Swarovski patented a machine that could cut glass crystals with great precision. Swarovski crystals contain a lot of lead. The combination of the precise cut and the lead in the glass makes these crystals sparkle like diamonds.

Wood Beads

Wood beads are found in many shapes, from simple to ornately carved.

Ceramic Beads

Ceramic beads can be colored with glazes, paints, enamel, or decals.

Shell Beads

Shell beads come in a variety of shapes, sizes, and colors. Shells are used whole or in pieces to create unique beads.

Pearl Beads

Pearls come from marine or freshwater mollusks, such as oysters or clams. Imitation pearls are made from glass or plastic.

Semiprecious Beads

Semiprecious stones are found in nature and removed from rock by mining. They are then shaped and polished into beads and other shapes.

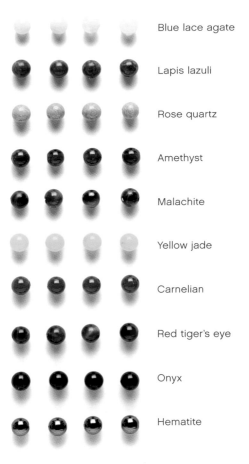

Blue lace agate

Lapis lazuli

Rose quartz

Amethyst

Malachite

Yellow jade

Carnelian

Red tiger's eye

Onyx

Hematite

Metal Beads

Gold and silver are very popular for fine jewelry. In addition, there are many more-affordable **base metals** that are used in jewelry making. Base metals are often coated with finishes that look like gold or silver.

Plastic Beads

Plastic is a versatile and inexpensive material for bead making. It can be tinted any color and molded into any shape imaginable.

Novelty Beads

Novelty beads are just plain fun! They can be made from any number of materials in any shape, size, or color.

Basic Bead Shapes

Round

Lentil

Barrel

Cube

Faceted

Star

Tube

Heart

Ring

Cylinder

Curved tube

Drop

Pillow or tab

Square cylinder

Cone

Pear

Disk

Flower

Bicone

Pyramid

Bead Sizes

Round beads are most often measured in millimeters. The sizing of seed beads is difficult and varies by manufacturer. With seed beads, the larger the number, the smaller the bead size.

Round Bead Sizes

2mm 3mm 4mm 5mm 6mm 7mm 8mm

9mm 10mm 11mm 12mm 13mm

Seed Bead Sizes

6

8

10

11

15

Bugle Sizes

1

2

3

4

5

How Many Beads Do You Need?

Use the chart below to determine the number of beads needed for a 16-inch necklace.

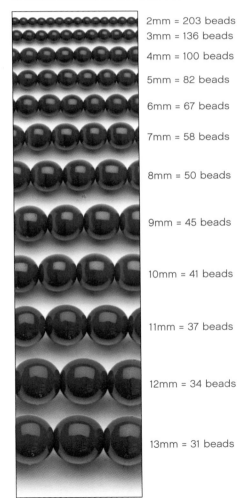

2mm = 203 beads
3mm = 136 beads
4mm = 100 beads
5mm = 82 beads
6mm = 67 beads
7mm = 58 beads
8mm = 50 beads
9mm = 45 beads
10mm = 41 beads
11mm = 37 beads
12mm = 34 beads
13mm = 31 beads

Findings

When making beaded jewelry, you will often need findings. Findings are the metal components used to make jewelry. Findings can be made from gold, silver, and less-expensive **base metals**. Decorative findings really add something special to a piece of jewelry.

Earring Findings

Most earring findings are for pierced ears. There are also clip earrings for those without pierced ears.

French hooks, or fishhooks, have a loop to which beads are attached.

Post earrings are available with a loop for attaching beads.

Clips and screw earrings are used for non-pierced ears.

Head Pins

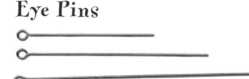

Head pins are made of wire that is flat at one end to prevent beads from slipping off.

Eye Pins

Eye pins have a loop at one end. The loop can be used to attach other beads.

Clasps

Clasps are used to fasten bracelets and necklaces and come in a wide variety.

Barrel clasps

Toggle clasps

Hook-and-eye clasps

Spring-ring clasps

Lobster claw clasps

Tube and slide-lock clasps

Safety, or fishhook, clasps

Jump Rings

A jump ring is a ring of metal that may be open or closed. They come in many sizes and are often used with spring-ring clasps. Jump rings should be opened sideways rather than pulled apart.

Crimps

Crimps are used to secure the ends of threads. Most clasps or jump rings attach to them.

French crimps are small metal tubes. Thread is passed through to form a loop. The crimp is then squeezed flat to secure the thread.

Tools & Supplies

The beaded jewelry projects in this book do not require many tools. As you become more interested in bead projects, you may want some specialized tools. These can help to accomplish more difficult techniques.

Scissors

It is important to have a sharp pair of scissors. Sometimes you may need to cut threads very precisely. Thin, sharp blades work best.

Needles

Sometimes you will need to use a needle. A beading needle is usually very fine and flexible. It is made to go through a bead more than one time. A size 12 needle is usually used for working with seed beads. A good technique for threading the small hole of the needle is to place the thread between your thumb and forefinger and guide the needle over the thread. It could be called "needling the thread" instead of "threading the needle."

Pliers

Pliers are needed for some of the projects in this book. You may find it easier to work with small tools so you can be close to your work. If you don't have what you need around the house, you can find special tools at a bead store.

Needle-nose pliers that are flat on the inside are used for flattening crimps, opening and closing jump rings, and attaching rings.

Round-nose pliers are used for forming loops.

Wire cutters are used for trimming and cutting head pins, eye pins, and beading wire. Some pliers have a built-in wire cutter.

Thread

Consider what type of thread suits the beads you have selected. The thread must be strong enough to support the weight of the beads. It needs to be thin enough to pass through the holes in the beads.

Polyester thread is available in many colors and diameters. Size B Nymo™ beading thread is often used for seed bead projects.

Nylon-coated wire is made of fine threads of wire covered by a layer of nylon. It is good for sharp or heavy beads as it won't fray. It is often called tiger tail wire. Some brands are more flexible and less prone to kinking than others.

Wire is also used for beading. Memory wire holds its original shape.

Cord is available in many colors and diameters. It can be made from leather, linen, cotton, and various imitation products. Cord is best used for larger beads.

Other Tools

There are other items that can make beading easier. Trays or jar lids hold various types of beads. Felt can be used for a work surface so that the beads don't roll onto the floor. Thread conditioners are used to bind thread fibers and prevent fraying.

Designing with Beads

Now you've had a glimpse of the tools, supplies, findings, and a few of the types of beads available. It is time to design your necklace or bracelet. Before your trip to the bead store, have in mind what you intend to make. How long will it be? How many beads do you need? What kind of pattern will you have? Following are a few tips to help you determine what you need.

Determine the Length

One of the great things about making your own jewelry is that you can **customize** it to fit you perfectly. Use a string to measure around your wrist or neck to determine the perfect length for your project. You will need thread for that length plus about four inches (10 cm) for making knots and attaching clasps.

Choosing the Beads

What is the mood you want to create with your piece? Are you making a necklace for a special occasion or to match a particular outfit? You may want to highlight a special bead.

Go to the bead store and look through the beads. You may find some that you "just have to" include. Work with those first and find other beads that complement them. Sometimes you can buy beads by the gram from a box of mixed beads. This can be a fun way to surround your special beads.

How Many Beads?

The bead board is a wonderful design tool that will also show how many beads you need. Most bead boards have grooves in them shaped like a necklace. There are measurements on the sides that show the length of a piece. Beads are placed in the grooves so they won't roll around while you design your jewelry. It makes it much easier to see your design before you string it.

If you use a bead board at the bead store, you'll know just how many beads to purchase. However, you should always get a few extra beads. You may change your pattern while you are working. You may decide to make matching earrings. And once you start beading, it's hard to stop. There will always be a use for those extra beads later!

The Design

There are many ways to approach your design. You can create a pattern with a small number of beads and repeat it over the length of your piece. A graduated pattern is made with the largest bead in the center. The other beads get smaller toward the clasp. Or you can just mix different shapes, colors, and sizes of beads to make a pleasing pattern.

Here are some examples of patterns that use the same beads to create different effects.

Memory Wire Bracelet

This is a quick and easy project for anyone. You can make it whatever length you want to. Almost any size bead will work on this wire bracelet!

What You Need

- Memory wire
- 12 to 23 inches (30 to 58 cm) of beads
- Marker
- Wire cutter
- Round-nose pliers

18

1 Wrap the memory wire around your wrist two or three times. Mark the wire at the place you want to cut it. Be careful, the ends of the wire may be sharp. Using the wire cutters, cut the wire at your mark.

2 Using the round-nose pliers, bend the end of the wire into a loop. The loop is so your beads will stay on.

3 This is the fun part! Start putting your beads on the wire. You can use your bead board to plan the order of your beads. Or, just slip the beads on the wire. Alternate colors and sizes of beads in any pattern you like.

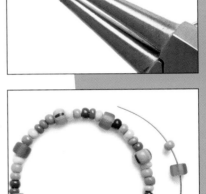

4 Fill the wire with beads, leaving about three-eighths inch (1 cm) of wire. Use the round-nose pliers to make a finishing loop. You're done!

Necklace on a Cord

This simple necklace can be worn by boys and girls alike.
The knots that form the closure are adjustable, so the
necklace can be any size. Just remember to select beads
that fit on the cord you select.

What You Need

- 32 to 36 inches (81 to 92 cm) of leather or imitation leather cord
- 6 to 8 inches (15 to 21 cm) of beads that have holes large enough to fit on the cord you select
- Scissors

How Many Beads?

Use the bead design board shown on page 17 to determine the amount of beads needed.

1 String the beads on the cord to the desired length. The closure is adjustable. Leave space at the back of the necklace to adjust the size.

2 Hold the two ends together so the beads fall to the center. Tie a knot next to the last bead on each side. This will secure the beads in place.

3 Bring one end of the cord to the opposite side. With the loose cord, tie an overhand knot around the cord as shown. Repeat this on the other side. Tighten the knots. Tie another overhand knot on each side for a more secure closure. Trim off any excess cord, leaving a small tail. Slip the necklace over your head and adjust it to a comfortable size.

Beaded Necklace

A beaded necklace can be as plain or as fancy as the beads you select. The length of the necklace is also up to you. You may want a choker or a longer necklace. This project is a loose-fitting choker with a charm as the centerpiece.

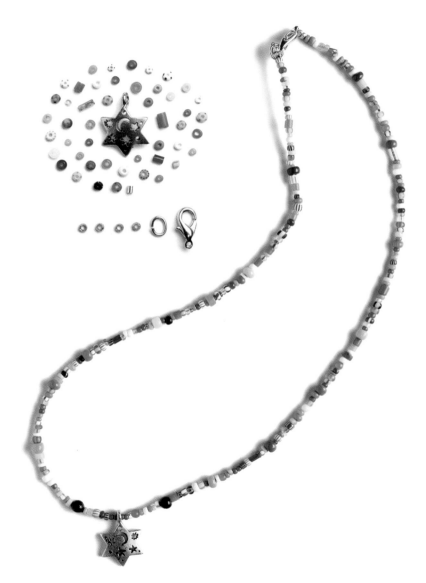

What You Need

- 18 to 24 inches (46 to 61 cm) of flexible tiger tail beading wire
- Seed beads in various sizes and colors
- Lobster claw clasp and jump ring
- 4 French crimps that match the color of the clasp
- Wire cutters
- Needle-nose pliers

1. Cut the beading wire. Slide two French crimps on one end of your wire. Pass the end of the wire through the loop on the clasp and back through the two crimps.

2. Use the needle-nose pliers to flatten the crimps. Cut the wire tail to about a half inch (1 cm).

3. Slide the first beads on the main wire and over the wire tail. String the rest of the beads. Once you have all the beads on, check the length. Adjust the amount of beads as necessary.

4. Put two crimps on the end of the wire. Run the wire through the jump ring, back through the crimps, then back through the last few beads. Pull to remove any slack in the necklace. Flatten the crimps and trim the wire tail.

Beaded Bracelet

This bracelet project uses the same finishing technique as the beaded necklace. However, it uses a different type of clasp.

What You Need

- 12 inches (30 cm) of flexible tiger tail beading wire
- Beads in various sizes and colors
- Toggle clasp
- 4 French crimps that match the color of the clasp
- Wire cutters
- Needle-nose pliers

1 Cut the beading wire. Slide two French crimps on one end of the wire. Pass the end of the wire through the loop on the clasp and back through the two crimps.

2 Use the needle-nose pliers to flatten the crimps. Cut the wire tail to about a half inch (1 cm). Slide the first beads on the wire and over the wire tail. String the rest of the beads. Check the length. Adjust the amount of beads as necessary.

3 Put the two remaining crimps on the end of the bracelet. Run the wire through the jump ring and back through the crimps.

4 Run the remaining wire through the last few beads. Trim the wire so that the end is hidden under the beads. Pull so there is no slack in your bracelet. Flatten the crimps.

Daisy Chain Necklace

The daisy chain is an easy way to use seed beads to create a really cool necklace or bracelet. With seed beads available in a variety of colors, you can make a necklace to go with anything!

What You Need

- Size 11 seed beads
- Thread
- Size 10 beading needle
- Barrel or other clasp
- Scissors

Tip

After tying on a clasp, dab a bit of clear nail polish on the knot to secure it.

Measure about 20 inches (51 cm) of thread. Thread the needle. Wrap the thread through the clasp several times. Tie two or three knots, repeat, then trim the thread tail.

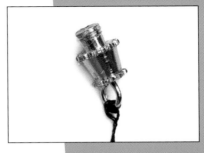

String seven beads on the thread. Then string on six beads to form the daisy. Bring the needle back through the first bead in the daisy. Pull the thread while holding the circle until it snugs up against the other beads.

String on the center bead and pass the needle through the bead opposite the first bead of the circle.

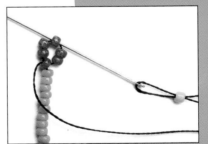

Add three beads and repeat until the necklace is the desired length. At the end of the necklace, add seven beads. Attach the clasp. Run the thread back through the last seven beads. Trim the excess thread.

Beaded Ring

This simple ring is easy
to make. You can create
variations by using
different beads.

What You Need

- Size 11 seed beads
- A few slightly larger beads
  for the links
- 26- or 28-gauge beading wire
- Wire cutters

1 Cut about ten inches (25 cm) of wire and bend it in half. Do this gently so you don't kink the wire. Add five beads to each side. To make the first link, string one bead on both wires. This bead closes the link.

2 Add five more seed beads to each wire. Then slip another large bead over both wires. Repeat until the ring fits around your finger. End on the single bead that closes the link.

3 To finish the ring, put both ends of the wire through the loop at the starting end. Pull the wires until the beads fit together snugly.

4 Thread the wire back through the large bead. Wrap it around the wire on the other side of the large bead. Wrap tightly two or three times and trim off the excess wire.

Stretchy Bracelet

This may be the easiest bracelet to make. However, it can be as elegant or as fun as you want to make it!

What You Need

- Beads of your choice
- Elastic beading thread. Select a size that will fit through the beads.
- Scissors

1 Cut about nine inches (23 cm) of elastic beading thread and string on the beads.

2 Wrap the strand around your wrist to check the length. Tie a square knot as shown below.

3 Make three or more single strands. Then string a final strand. Wrap it around the other strands. Add beads as necessary. Tie the knot and trim off the excess thread.

Glossary

base metal – any non-precious metal, such as zinc, copper, nickel, or brass.

customize – to make something to personal specifications.

facet – a flat, polished surface of a cut gem or glass.

frost – to produce a slightly roughened finish. Frosted beads are created by tumbling them in an abrasive substance.

iridescent – having a rainbow-like appearance.

lampwork bead – a bead made by hand using a glass rod heated by a lamp or burner.

millefiori – Italian for "one thousand flowers." This ornamental glass is made by fusing together multicolored glass canes and then slicing it.

opaque – material that does not allow light to pass through.

semiprecious – of less value than a precious stone.

Web Sites

To learn more about beaded jewelry, visit ABDO Publishing Company on the World Wide Web at **www.abdopub.com**. Web sites about beaded jewelry are featured on our Book Links page. These links are routinely monitored and updated to provide the most current information available.

Index

B

bead board 17, 19
bead shapes 10
bead sizes 11
bead-making methods 5
beaded ring 28
bugle beads 7

C

ceramic beads 8
chevron beads 6
choker 22
clasps 13, 16
crimps 13, 14, 22, 23, 24, 25

D

daisy chain 26
design 16, 17, 20

E

earring findings 12
eye pins 12, 14

F

findings 12, 16
frosted beads 7, 31
furnace glass beads 6

G

glass beads 5, 6, 7

H

head pins 12, 14
history of beads 5

I

iridescent beads 7, 31
iris beads 7

J

jump rings 13, 14

L

lampwork beads 6, 31

M

memory wire 15, 18, 19
metal beads 9
metallic beads 7
millefiori beads 6, 31
molded glass beads 6

N

needles 14
novelty beads 9

O

opaque beads 7, 31

P

pearl beads 8
plastic beads 9
pliers 14, 18, 19, 22, 23, 24, 25

R

rocailles 7

S

seed beads 5, 7, 11, 14, 22, 26, 28, 29
semiprecious beads 8, 31
shell beads 8
silver-lined beads 7
stretchy bracelet 30
Swarovski glass beads 7
Swarovski, Daniel 7

T

thread 13, 14, 15, 16, 26, 27, 29, 30
transparent beads 7

W

wood beads 8